GROW
YOUR OWN
RECIPES

compiled by
Simon Haseltine

*Illustrated with
retro garden images
by Martin Wiscombe*

SALMON

Index

Allotment Chilli Chutney 32
Apple Meringue Pie 45
Balsamic Roasted Vegetables 10
BBQ Vegetable Kebabs 24
Berry Cake 46
Beetroot and Apple Crumble 43
Broccoli and Spinach Bake 13
Butternut Squash and Cheese Curry 8
Canadian Pumpkin Pie 27
Cauliflower and Broccoli Cheese with
  Crispy Bacon 34
Chilli Winter Soup 3
Christmas Brussels Sprouts 15
Cider Glazed Vegetables 18
Courgette and Ham Pasta with
  Homemade Tomato Sauce 35
Moroccan Vegetable Tagine 23
Picnic Quiche 30

Ratatouille 21
Rhubarb and Strawberry Jam 40
Rhubarb Marmalade 42
Sausage and Leek Pie 39
Sizzling Vegetable Chilli 6
Spinach Wraps 7
Spring Time Stew 38
Stilton Soup 5
Stir Fry Cabbage 14
Stuffed Marrow 11
Stuffed Peppers 29
Summer Iced Tea 47
The Ultimate "On Toast" 31
Vegetable Cornish Pasty 19
Vegetable Lasagne 22
Vegetable Rosti 16
Vegetable Tart 26
Warming Winter Stew 37

Printed and published by J. Salmon Ltd., Sevenoaks, England © Copyright
All images copyright © Martin Wiscombe

Chilli Winter Soup

Warming and spicy for a chilly winter's day…

1 onion (chopped)   2 potatoes (cubed)
1 lb. vegetables
(try a seasonal mixture of swede, carrots, parsnips, cabbage, leeks, kale –
all cut into small pieces)
1 garlic clove   1 red chilli (deseeded and diced)
½ cup porridge oats   Pinch mixed herbs
1½ pints vegetable stock (plus a little extra water)
Salt and pepper (to taste)   Oil

In a large saucepan, fry the onion and garlic in some oil for 5 minutes until soft. Then add all the prepared vegetables and stir through the onion mixture for a few minutes. Add the herbs and oats, stir once then pour over the stock. Bring to a boil and simmer very gently for around 20 minutes until the vegetables are tender – the slower you simmer then the greater the flavour. Remove from the heat and cool a little, then liquidise until the soup is smooth. Store in fridge for a few hours until required, then return to the pan and heat through. Serve with some homemade buttered bread. Serves 4.

Stilton Soup

A festive way to use up all your Stilton cheese…

1 lb. potatoes (peeled and cubed)
1 large floret broccoli (shredded – stalk chopped)
1 hunk of Stilton cheese (around 4 oz.)
1 large onion (chopped)   2 cloves garlic (crushed)
1 ltr. vegetable stock   150 ml. cream
Salt and pepper (to taste)
Knob of butter and oil

Heat the butter and oil and a large saucepan and add the chopped onion and garlic and gently cook for around 5 minutes until soft. Add the cubed potatoes, broccoli (and chopped stalk) and stock, bring to the boil and then simmer for 15 minutes or until the potatoes are soft. Remove from heat and cool before blending in a food processor until smooth. Return to the saucepan and add the cream and crumbled Stilton and heat gently until the cheese has melted, stirring all the time. Add salt and pepper to taste and serve with a large chunk of crusty bread. Serves 4.

Sizzling Vegetable Chilli

A spicy vegetarian alternative to the traditional chilli…

2 onions (chopped)   2 cloves garlic (crushed)
1 can chopped tomatoes   4 tomatoes (skinned and diced)
1 red chilli (deseeded and chopped)   8 oz. mushrooms (sliced)
1 green pepper (diced)
8 oz. mixed vegetables
(choose from courgette, butternut squash, sweet potato – all diced – peas, sweet corn)
1 can kidney beans   Water (as required)   Oil

Sauté the onions and chilli in the oil for 5 minutes, then add the garlic and cook for a further minute. Add the remaining ingredients (except the kidney beans) and simmer for 20 minutes until the vegetables are tender, adding a little water for the required consistency. Add the drained kidney beans and simmer for a further 5 minutes, then serve with rice or over a baked potato. Serves 4.

Spinach Wraps

A colourful and nutritious wrap…

Around 30 spinach leaves	**4 oz. Cheddar cheese (grated)**
8 oz. mushrooms (sliced)	**4 wraps**
Small tin sweet corn	**Olive oil**
4 tomatoes (skinned and chopped)	**Tub of Greek yogurt**

Sauté the mushrooms and tomatoes in the oil for 5 minutes until tender, then add the sweet corn and spinach leaves. Stir gently over a medium heat until the spinach leaves have wilted. Immediately serve in wraps together with a dollop of Greek yogurt and a sprinkling of Cheddar cheese. Serves 4.

Butternut Squash and Cheese Curry

A mouth-watering combination of curry and tangy cheese…

**1 onion (chopped)   1 lb. butternut squash (peeled and cubed)
8 oz. cauliflower (small florets)   8 oz. broccoli (small florets)
4 cloves garlic (crushed)   1½ pt. chicken stock
1 red chilli pepper (deseeded and diced)
4 tbsp. curry powder (or to taste)
8 oz. very strong Cheddar cheese (large cubes)
Handful coriander leaves   Oil**

Sauté the onion and chilli in a little oil for 5 minutes then add the garlic, butternut squash and curry powder and stir for a further minute to mix all the spices with the vegetables. Add the stock and bring to the boil and simmer for 10 minutes. Then add the cauliflower and broccoli florets and simmer for a further 10 minutes until tender. Turn off the heat and ladle into a serving dish and add the cubed cheese and coriander leaves. Serve immediately with rice, the cheese will be tangy and stringy. Serves 4.

Balsamic Roasted Vegetables

A colourful combination of seasonal vegetables…

1 small pumpkin (chunked)   **1 sweet potato (chunked)**
2 courgettes (chunked)   **3 tbsp. balsamic vinegar**
1 red pepper (chopped)   **2 sprigs of rosemary**
1 large parsnip (chunked)   **½ cup olive oil**

Place the prepared vegetables in a roasting pan and add the balsamic vinegar and olive oil and stir to combine all the ingredients. Add the sprigs of rosemary, cover with foil and roast in a hot oven at Gas 6/200C° for 20 minutes. Remove foil and turn the vegetables. Return to the oven and roast for a further 10 to 20 minutes until tender. Serve on their own with a chunk of bread for lunch or with chicken for supper. Serves 4.

Stuffed Marrow

A delicious and filling supper dish…

1 medium sized marrow	4 handfuls grated Cheddar
1 lb. beef mince meat	1 beef stock cube
1 large onion (chopped)	½ cup porridge oats
4 cloves garlic (crushed)	A little flour
6 tomatoes (skinned and finely chopped)	A little water

Skin the marrow and cut into 4 thick slices or around 2 inches deep. Scoop out the seeds and place on a baking tray. Meanwhile, sauté the onion and tomatoes in a frying pan for 5 minutes until they have softened, then add the mince and garlic and brown for a further 5 minutes. Crumble in the stock cube and sprinkle in the oats and flour and cook for 2 minutes, stirring all the time. Add a little water if required to form a thick consistency. Spoon the mince mixture into each of the 4 marrow rings and place a foil lid over the tray. Bake in a hot oven Gas 6/200C°, for 50 minutes and then remove the foil lid and crumble the cheese over the top of each. Return to the oven (without the foil lid) for a further 10 minutes. Serve with some colourful carrots and salad potatoes. Serves 4.

Broccoli and Spinach Bake

An easy supper dish for all the family…

1 large onion (chopped)
1 lb. broccoli (cut into florets)
Good handful spinach leaves (stalks removed)
2 carrots (grated)
4 large tomatoes (skinned and quartered)
3 oz. butter   3 oz. plain flour   1 pt. milk
4 oz. Cheddar cheese (grated)   Oil

Fry the onion in a little oil for 5 minutes until they are soft. In a saucepan, melt the butter and stir in the flour and heat through over a low heat for 2 minutes. Gradually pour over the milk, stirring all the time, and simmer for a few minutes until the sauce has thickened. Turn off the heat and fold through the grated cheese. Meanwhile, steam the broccoli for around 10 minutes then place in a small ovenproof dish. Add the tomatoes, spinach and grated carrots and pour over the cheese sauce. Bake in the oven at Gas 7/220C°, for 10 minutes or until the top is golden brown. Serves 4.

For an alternative, add flaked salmon, cubes of ham or crispy bacon to the broccoli before pouring over the cheese sauce.

Stir Fry Cabbage

Even the humble cabbage can be made exciting…

1 lb. cabbage (shredded)
1 small onion (diced)
2 cloves garlic (crushed)
2 tbsp. soya sauce
Oil

Heat the oil in a wok or large frying pan and add the onion and garlic. Stir fry for a minute, then add the cabbage and stir fry for a further 2 minutes. Add the soya sauce and cook for 3 minutes, stirring all the time, until the cabbage is tender. Serve as an accompaniment to your favourite Chinese dishes. Serves 4.

Alternative: for a one-dish meal, add some strips of cooked chicken and a handful of beansprouts at the same time as the cabbage and double the soya sauce.

Christmas Brussels Sprouts

A very festive alternative...

1 lb. Brussels sprouts (peeled and shredded)
4 oz. butter
1 large red onion (diced)
4 oz. chestnuts (cooked and chopped)
Salt and pepper to taste
Oil

Melt the butter in a large pan with a little oil and sauté the onion for 5 minutes or until soft. In a second pan, blanch the shredded Brussels sprouts for a minute in boiling water, then drain. Add the sprouts and chestnuts to the onion mixture, stir to coat with the oil and butter and cook for 5 minutes, stirring some of the time. Season with salt and pepper and serve. Serves 4.

Vegetable Rosti

A very tasty combination of three humble vegetables…

4 large potatoes (peeled and grated)
1 large parsnip (peeled and grated)
1 carrot (peeled and grated)
Pinch dried herbs (or a little fresh rosemary – chopped)
2 oz. butter
Salt and pepper to taste
Oil

Place the grated potatoes, carrot and parsnip into a clean linen towel and wring dry. Place in a bowl and fold in the herbs and a little salt and pepper and form into rough scone shapes. Heat the butter and a little oil in a large frying pan, add the potato and parsnip cakes and fry on each side for around 5 minutes until they are golden brown. Serve the Rosti with a poached egg for lunch or as a side vegetable for supper. Serves 4.

ROOT VEGETABLES

Carrots.—Sow a small fra[me]
and Early Scarlet Horn;

—Sow Guer[n]
from eightee[n]

Beetroot.—Sow [e]arly Frame and
sowings will affo[rd] a useful
sow again under [g]lass next

Radishes.—Sow Wood's
Scarlet on a slight hotbed, a[nd]
open air. The three sowings

Turnips.—S[ow]
Keep down all
growing crops sw[...]

Beetroot *Radish* *Turnip*

Cider Glazed Vegetables

A delicious supper party dish…

2 peppers (one red, one green – deseeded and sliced)
2 medium red onions (sliced)
2 courgettes (thickly sliced)
2 carrots (thickly sliced)
½ cauliflower (broken into florets)
1 eating apple (sliced)
3 cloves garlic (crushed)
7 fl. oz. cider   Sprigs of rosemary
Oil   Salt and pepper to taste

Pre-heat oven to Gas 6/200C°, and place prepared vegetables, apple and herbs into a roasting tin and drizzle with oil. Pour cider into tin, season with salt and pepper, cover with foil and bake for 40 minutes until tender. Remove the foil lid and return to the oven for 10 further minutes to brown. Serve with a grilled pork chop and some homemade apple sauce. Serves 4.

Vegetable Cornish Pasty

A vegetarian pasty using a selection of seasonal vegetables…

1 carrot   1 small parsnip   1 stalk celery
1 small swede   1 small onion   1 clove garlic (crushed)
4 oz. cooked chestnuts (tinned or vacuum packed)
1 egg (beaten)   ½ tsp. nutmeg
Pinch dried herbs   Splash red wine
Oil and butter for frying   Milk for brushing
Pre-made short crust pastry

Prepare all the vegetables by cutting into small cubes and gently fry in the oil and butter with the garlic and herbs for 10 minutes. Chop the chestnuts and add to the vegetable mixture, along with the egg and a splash of red wine, stirring over the heat for a further minute. Roll out the pastry and cut four small plate-size circles. Dollop a quarter of the vegetable mixture on one half of the pastry circle and fold over, crimping the edges. Brush the pasties with milk and bake in an oven Gas 6/200C° for 20 minutes or until golden brown. Serve with chunky chips and lashings of your favourite brown sauce. Serves 4.

Ratatouille

A great amalgamation of colours and flavours…

1 large onion (chopped)
4 cloves garlic (crushed)
2 small courgettes (chopped)
8 large tomatoes (skinned and chopped)
Pinch mixed herbs
Splash water
Oil

Sauté the onion and garlic in the oil for 5 minutes, then add the remaining ingredients. Stir to mix with the oil and onion, then gently cook for 30 minutes until tender, adding a splash of water to keep the mixture from getting too dry. Serve dolloped over a baked potato for lunch or as a supper side dish. Serves 4.

Vegetable Lasagne

A vegetarian alternative to a family favourite…

Selection of seasonal vegetables:
1 large onion, 2 medium courgettes, 1 small aubergine, 6 large beefsteak tomatoes
(all cut into small chunks)
1 green pepper   8 oz. mushrooms   6 cloves garlic (chopped)
8 fl. oz. vegetable stock   3 fl. oz. white wine   4 tbsp. tomato purée
1 pt. béchamel sauce   Packet lasagne sheets (around 12 needed)
4 oz. grated cheese   Oil and salt

Heat the oven to Gas 6/200C°, and place the prepared vegetables, peppers, mushrooms and garlic in a roasting tray. Drizzle with oil, add salt and roast for 30 minutes until tender. Mix the tomato purée, wine and stock together and pour over the roasted vegetables, stirring gently. Place in the oven for a further 5 minutes. Remove from oven and spread enough of the vegetable mixture in a greased lasagne dish to cover the base and cover with sheets of lasagne. Pour over some of the béchamel sauce and repeat until you finish with a layer of sauce. Sprinkle over the cheese and return the oven (reduced to Gas 4/180C°) for 40 minutes. Serve with a fresh green salad and some garlic bread. Serves 4.

Moroccan Vegetable Tagine

A colourful dish using up late summer vegetables…

**1 courgette (chunked)   1 large carrot (chunked)   1 sweet potato (chunked)
1 butternut squash (chunked)   1 large red onion (sliced)
1 red pepper (chunked)   4 large tomatoes (skinned and quartered)
2 cloves garlic (crushed)   1 tsp. coriander   1 tsp. ground cumin
1 tsp. paprika   1 tsp. cinnamon   1 tsp. allspice
1 tsp. salt   1 pint hot vegetable stock   Olive oil
1 tsp. Parmesan cheese (grated Cheddar cheese will do)**

In a frying pan, fry the onion and garlic in some oil for around 5 minutes until soft. Place the vegetables and onion mixture in a tagine and sprinkle over all the spices. Pour over the hot vegetable stock, cover with the tagine lid and place in the oven at Gas 4/180C°, to roast for around 40 minutes, or until tender. Remove from oven and gently stir in the Parmesan cheese before serving with couscous, which can be cooked at the same time. Serves 4.

As an alternative to a tagine, use a large casserole dish with a lid.

BBQ Vegetable Kebabs

A wonderful addition to a sizzling summer BBQ…

2 courgettes (large cubes)
1 red and 1 green pepper (large slices)
12 button mushrooms
Slice of pumpkin (cubed)
Cherry tomatoes

2 tbsp. runny honey
1 lemon (juice)
4 tbsp. olive oil
Basil leaves
Halloumi or feta cheese (chunks)

Place the prepared vegetables on skewer sticks, alternating colours, textures and flavours, placing the cheese chunks next to the mushrooms. Whisk the honey, olive oil, lemon juice and basil leaves and drizzle most of the marinade over the vegetable kebabs. Place over the BBQ coals and grill for around 20 minutes until tender, adding the remaining marinade half way through cooking. Serves 4.

Vegetable Tart

A summertime luncheon dish…

1 pack (500 g.) of puff pastry
Selection of peppers (2 in total – sliced)
2 courgettes (sliced)   1 red onion (chopped)
1 garlic clove (finely chopped)   2 tablespoons tomato purée
Handful of chopped herbs (parsley and basil work well)
Olive oil   Salt and pepper to taste
Pinch of dried mixed herbs

Pre-heat your oven to Gas 6/200C°, and grease a baking sheet. Place the prepared vegetables and herbs on the baking sheet, drizzle with olive oil and season to taste with salt and pepper, then bake in the oven for 20 minutes. Remove from the oven and put vegetables aside. Roll out the puff pastry to a 1 foot square and place on the baking tray. Stir together the garlic, dried mixed herbs and tomato purée and spread on the puff pastry, leaving about an inch margin all round. Place the baked vegetables on the tomato purée, sprinkle with the parsley and return to the oven for a further 20 minutes. Serve hot or cold with the basil leaves and a tomato and olive oil salad. Serves 4.

Canadian Pumpkin Pie

A taste of Canada in the fall…

Sweet short crust pastry (6 oz. flour – 9 inches)
1 lb. pumpkin flesh (cubed)
2 eggs plus 1 egg yolk (beaten)
3 oz. soft dark brown sugar
1 tsp. cinnamon
½ tsp. each nutmeg, allspice, cloves, ginger
10 fl. oz. double cream

Blind bake the pastry in a 9 inch pie or flan dish. Then steam the pumpkin until tender and allow to cool slightly. Place through a sieve and then squeeze the flesh to remove any excess water. In a pan, gently bring to the boil the cream, sugar and spices. Place the egg mixture into a bowl and add the hot cream and whisk briefly before adding the sieved pumpkin, whisking for a further minute to combine all the ingredients. Pour the filling into the prepared pie case and bake in an oven Gas 4/180C°, for 40 minutes or until golden brown. Cool on a wire rack and serve cold with cream. Serves 4.

Stuffed Peppers

A stunning combination of colour and flavour…

4 peppers (a combination of colours will look stunning)
800 g. couscous
10 each dried apricots and prunes (chopped)
2 pts. vegetable stock (hot)
1 orange (juice and grated rind)
8 tbsp. runny honey
8 tbsp. herbs *(try a combination of mint, basil, parsley etc – all finely chopped)*
2 garlic cloves (crushed)   Olive oil

Slice the tops off the peppers and deseed them. Place on a baking tray and drizzle with olive oil and place in the oven at Gas 4/180C°, for 10 minutes or until they turn golden brown. Meanwhile, soak the couscous, dried fruit and garlic in the hot stock and orange juice and set aside for 5 minutes until all the liquid has been absorbed. Fluff up the couscous and fold in the herbs, grated orange rind and honey. Spoon the mixture into the roasted peppers and return to the oven for a few further minutes to crisp the top of the stuffing. Serve with a crispy green salad. Serves 4.

Picnic Quiche

A perfect picnic dish to accompany any summer's day outing…

1 pre-baked 9 inch quiche case	1 small red onion (chopped)
1 large broccoli floret (shredded)	4 eggs
1 courgette (chopped)	¼ pt. single cream
2 large tomatoes (skinned and chopped)	¼ tsp. ground nutmeg

Pinch dried herbs

Place vegetable filling in the pre-baked quiche case. Beat the eggs together in a bowl, then whisk in the cream, nutmeg and herbs. Pour over the quiche filling and bake in a preheated oven Gas 4/180C°, for 40 minutes until the centre has set (test by inserting a knife – if clean, then the quiche has set). Set aside to cool and serve on a picnic with a tomato salad and a glass of chilled wine. Serves 4.

The Ultimate "On Toast"

Such a simple but tasty lunchtime dish…

12 tomatoes (halved)	**4 free range eggs**
2 cloves garlic (crushed)	**Olive oil**
Bunch of basil leaves	**Salt and white pepper**
Handful of sunflower seeds	**Buttered toast and Marmite**

Deskin and slice the tomatoes. Add tomatoes, garlic, sunflower seeds and the basil to a roasting pan and drizzle over the olive oil, stir once to mix all the ingredients. Roast in a hot oven Gas 6/200C°, for 25 minutes, when the tomatoes will start to colour. Turn out onto 4 slices of buttered toast and Marmite and season with salt and pepper. Meanwhile, fry 4 eggs on the hob and gently place on top of the tomatoes. Serves 4.

Allotment Chilli Chutney

A great way to use up your glut of vegetables…

**2 onions (diced)   1 lb. tomatoes (skinned and diced)
1 lb. courgettes (diced)
2 cooking apples (skinned and diced)
4 cloves garlic (crushed)
1 red chilli (deseeded and finely chopped)
Handful of sultanas   8 oz. brown sugar
1 tsp. mustard powder
Small (½ inch) piece root ginger (grated)
½ pt. spiced malt vinegar**

Place the prepared vegetables and sugar in a large saucepan and stir in the vinegar. Bring slowly to the boil and simmer for around 2 hours, or until the chutney is dark and thick and no liquid remains. Pour into sterilised jars and seal immediately. Allow to mature for 4 weeks before eating with your favourite cheese or cold meats. Makes around 2 lbs. of chutney.

Cauliflower and Broccoli Cheese with Crispy Bacon

A colourful and tangy lunchtime meal…

**1 large cauliflower   1 large broccoli stalk
1 oz. flour   3 oz. Cheddar cheese (grated)
½ pint milk   1 oz. butter   1 tsp. mustard powder
Paprika (sprinkle)
4 rashers bacon (diced small – cooked to a crisp)**

Break the cauliflower and broccoli into florets and place in large saucepan of water. Bring to the boil and simmer for 10 minutes or until just tender. Remove from heat, drain and place in an ovenproof dish. Meanwhile, place the butter, mustard and flour in a small saucepan and melt over a low heat, then cook for a minute of two, stirring all the time. Gently add the milk and whisk until smooth, then add the grated cheese. Bring the sauce to a boil and simmer until it has thickened. Fold in the cooked bacon pieces and allow to warm through for a minute. Pour the cheese sauce over the vegetables and place in a hot oven Gas 6/200C°, for 10 minutes until the sauce is golden brown. Sprinkle with paprika and serve immediately. Serves 4.

Courgette and Ham Pasta with Homemade Tomato Sauce

Such an easy pasta sauce with no jars or tins…

2 medium-size courgettes (sliced)
4 oz. ham pieces (cubed)
8 large ripe tomatoes (skinned and cubed)
2 cloves garlic (crushed)
1 large red onion (diced)
Olive oil
Pinch mixed herbs
Water (around half a cup full)
1 lb. dried pasta

In a frying pan, sauté the onion, courgette slices and garlic for around 5 minutes until soft, then add the tomatoes, diced ham and herbs and gently fry for a further 10 minutes. Add a little water to gain the consistency as required. Meanwhile, cook the pasta in accordance to the pack instructions and drain. Fold the pasta into the tomato sauce mixture, heat through for a minute or two and serve. Serves 4.

Warming Winter Stew

This is one of my family's favourite winter comfort foods…

**1 lb. stewing steak (small cubes) 1 large onion (chunked)
1 red chilli pepper (deseeded and chopped)
Selection of winter vegetables – try 2 carrots, 2 potatoes, 1 small swede, 2 leeks,
2 courgettes, handful green beans (all chopped to small segments) or replace some with
equal proportions of butternut squash and sweet potato
Half a cup porridge oats Half a cup dried broth mix Pinch dried herbs
1 beef stock cube Water Oil Flour**

In a frying pan, gently fry the beef in a little oil until browned, then sprinkle with flour and turn a few times before placing in a slow cooker. Next, fry the onion and chilli in the remaining meat juices for a few minutes and add to the meat, together with all the prepared vegetables and dried broth mix. Make up 1 pt. of stock using the beef stock cube and dried herbs and pour over the stew. Sprinkle over the oats and gently stir together. Place lid over the slow cooker and cook on low for around 6 hours – stirring a few times and checking if any further water is required (always add hot water). Serve with a jacket potato and some winter greens. Serves 4.

Alternative cooking method: place stew in a large ovenproof dish with a lid and cook in the middle of a medium oven (Gas 4/180C°) for 2 hours.

Spring Time Stew

A fresh tasting stew with all the flavours of spring time…

1 lb. new potatoes (freshly dug, scrubbed and chunked)
1 large onion (sliced)
1 lb. spring vegetables *(choose a selection from baby carrots, baby leeks, peas, spring cabbage, purple sprouting broccoli – any large ones cut into large chunks)*
1 small red or green chilli (deseeded and thinly sliced)
1 garlic clove (crushed)
1½ pints vegetable stock
Handful seasonal herbs (chopped)
(try a combination of borage, chives, parsley, rosemary and even a few curry plant leaves for extra warmth)
Oil

Heat some oil in a large pan and fry the onion for around 5 minutes until soft, then add the crushed garlic and sliced chilli and fry for a few more minutes. Pour in the stock and add the potatoes, bring to the boil and simmer for 5 minutes. Add all the seasonal vegetables and simmer for a further 15 minutes until they are tender. Stir in the herbs and cook through for a few minutes before serving as a meal in itself. Serves 4.

Sausage and Leek Pie

This is my mum's recipe and reminds me of early January suppers using up the remaining leeks from dad's allotment

Short crust pastry (using 12 oz. plain flour)
2 leeks (chopped)
8 oz. sausage meat (good quality)
2 eggs
A little milk (just a splash)
Handful of Cheddar cheese (grated)

Make the pastry and divide into two portions. Roll out the first and line a shallow pie dish. Spread the sausage meet over the pastry and then add the chopped leeks. Take one egg and beat in a small bowl with a little milk and pour over the leeks. Sprinkle over the cheese. Roll out the second piece of pastry and place over the pie to form a lid. Beat the second egg and use to seal the edges of the pastry and brush over the lid. Make in a hot oven Gas 6/200C° for 20 minutes, then reduce the oven to Gas 4/180C° for a further 40 minutes. Serve piping hot with mash potato and seasonal vegetables. Serves 4.

Rhubarb and Strawberry Jam

A delicious jam and perfect on hot buttered toast…

2 lb. rhubarb (washed and cut into 2 inch pieces)
1 lb. strawberries (hulled and halved)
¼ pt. water
2 lemons (grated rind and juice)
3 lb. jam-making sugar

Place the rhubarb into a large pan and pour over the water and bring to the boil. Simmer gently for around 20 minutes, then add the strawberries, lemon rind and juice. Return to simmering point and add the sugar, stirring until the sugar has dissolved. Bring to the boil and boil rapidly until setting point has been reached (around 10 to 15 minutes). Cool slightly, stir and pour into sterilised jars and seal immediately.

Strawberry Jam

Rhubarb Marmalade

An unusual but tangy way to use up your rhubarb…

4 lb. rhubarb
2 lemons (rind only)
2 oranges (rind and juice)
½ inch ginger (grated)
½ pint liquid – the orange juice plus water
5 lb. jam-making sugar

Wash and trim the rhubarb into around 1 inch lengths. Put into a preserving pan, together with the water, orange juice, ginger and grated lemon rind and bring to the boil and simmer for 10 minutes. Add the sugar and boil rapidly until setting point has been reached, then ladle into sterilised jars and seal immediately. Makes around 6 lb.

Tip: To test for setting point, spoon a little marmalade onto a cold plate. If it wrinkles when pushed with the tip of your finger, then setting point has been reached.

Beetroot and Apple Crumble

An unusual combination and certainly the talking point of any supper party…

For the fruit:
1 lb. cooking apples (peeled, chopped and drizzled with lemon juice)
1 large beetroot (cooked – diced small)
4 oz. brown sugar

For the crumble:
3 oz. butter   4 oz. self-raising flour
2 oz. brown sugar (plus a little extra for sprinkling)
1 oz. porridge oats

Place the prepared apples in a saucepan and add half the sugar and simmer gently for 5 minutes. Pour into the base of a deep ovenproof dish and dot with the diced beetroot. Fold in the remaining sugar. Meanwhile, place the butter and flour into a bowl and rub together with your fingers until it looks like breadcrumbs. Add the oats and sugar and mix together. Pour the crumble over the fruit and sprinkle the top with a little brown sugar. Place in a pre-heated oven Gas 5/190C°, for around 30 minutes or until the crumble is golden brown. Serve with a dollop of cream or hot custard. Serves 4.

DELICIOUS APPLES

Cox's Orange Pipin

'A large and handsome fruit'

Apple Meringue Pie

A tasty alternative to the traditional lemon meringue pie…

Sweet short crust pastry (6 oz. flour – 9 inches)
6 tart eating apples (peeled, cored and sliced)
Handful dried fruit   2 oz. sugar   2 egg yolks (beaten)
1 lemon (grated rind and juice)   1 oz. butter

Meringue:
3 egg whites   ½ tsp. vanilla essence   6 oz. caster sugar

Cook the prepared apples and dried with a splash of water for 10 to 15 minutes or until soft, then remove from heat and drain any liquid. Then fold in the sugar, butter, flour, egg yolks and lemon and return to the heat for a further 5 minutes to cook through. Spoon the mixture into the prepared 9 inch pastry shell. To make the meringue, beat the egg whites with the vanilla essence until they form soft peaks, then add the caster sugar and beat until stiff. Spread the meringue over the apple mixture and bake in a cool oven Gas 2/150C°, for an hour or until the meringue is golden brown. Serves 4.

Berry Cake

An upside-down version of a very fruity cake…

**8 oz. self-raising flour   8 oz. butter   8 oz. caster sugar
1 oz. ground almonds   4 free range eggs
8 oz. mixed soft fruit
*(try a combination of strawberries, raspberries, blue berries,
blackberries – chopped and dusted with sugar)*
2 tbsp. golden syrup**

Grease and line an 8 inch cake tin and preheat your oven to Gas 4/180C°. Beat the sugar and butter together until fluffy, then gradually beat in the eggs, a little at a time. Fold in the flour and ground almonds and add a little water if too dry. Place the fruit at the bottom of the cake tin, spreading evenly over the base. Add the syrup over the fruit and carefully spoon the cake mixture over the top. Bake in the centre of the oven for 1 hour and check with a sharp knife whether the cake is cooked through. If the knife comes out wet, then bake for a further 10 minutes or so before testing again. Cool slightly in the tin, and then turn out, so that the tangy fruit layer is on top.

Alternative: stew 8 oz. gooseberries or rhubarb with 2 tbsp. brown sugar and use instead of the soft fruit and exclude the syrup. Serve hot with custard.

Summer Iced Tea

A refreshing non-alcoholic alternative to a summer Pimms...

1½ pints strong breakfast tea
1 can ginger beer
1 tbsp. sugar (or slightly more to taste)
1 lemon (juice only)
Soft fruit (around 12 pieces - halved)
Sprigs of mint

Make the tea and allow to cool. Pour into a large glass jug and add the fruit, sprigs of mint, sugar and lemon juice, stirring a few times. Add the ginger beer immediately prior to serving and pour over ice cubes in large glasses, ensuring equal proportions of fruit.

METRIC CONVERSIONS

The weights, measures and oven temperatures used in the preceding recipes can be easily converted to their metric equivalents. The conversions listed below are only approximate, having been rounded up or down as may be appropriate.

Weights

Avoirdupois	Metric
1 oz.	just under 30 grams
4 oz. (¼ lb.)	app. 115 grams
8 oz. (½ lb.)	app. 230 grams
1 lb.	454 grams

Liquid Measures

Imperial	Metric
1 tablespoon (liquid only)	20 millilitres
1 fl. oz.	app. 30 millilitres
1 gill (¼ pt.)	app. 145 millilitres
½ pt.	app. 285 millilitres
1 pt.	app. 570 millilitres
1 qt.	app. 1.140 litres

Oven Temperatures

	°Fahrenheit	Gas Mark	°Celsius
Slow	300	2	150
	325	3	170
Moderate	350	4	180
	375	5	190
	400	6	200
Hot	425	7	220
	450	8	230
	475	9	240

Flour as specified in these recipes refers to plain flour unless otherwise described.